CLASSROOM

DISCIPLINE

WITHOUT

CONFUSION

CLASSROOM DISCIPLINE WITHOUT CONFUSION

By

Joy Williams

Published by To His Glory Publishing Company, Inc.
111 Sunnydale Court
Lawrenceville, GA 30044
(770) 458-7947
www.tohisglorypublishing.com

Graphical Layout and Composition: Obasi Scott: Shepherds Loft LLC. www.shepherdsloft.com

Book is available at:
Amazon.com, BarnesandNoble.com, Borders.com etc.

International Standard Book Number: 0-9749802-2-6

DEDICATION

To the many men and women who teach the students
who challenge us all

CONTENTS

ACKNOWLEDGMENTS

*I would like to thank God for giving me
the strength and the vision to write this book*

*Thanks a million to
Mario O. Tyson (Desktop Publishing and editing work)
and to
H. Graphiks (cover illustration)
for your
dedicated and tireless efforts*

INTRODUCTION

In today's society, we have created a generation of children that have been empowered to know their rights. They have been informed through television, radio, newspapers, magazines and the Internet that they are not only children, but also smaller human beings that have certain privileges. Society may have meant it for the good of the children, but the children have used and abused these rights.

We have been very careful not to hurt the children's feelings, label them, ignore them, disrespect them, or expect too much from them. With this mindset, we have made these children "mini gods"! The children now feel they can do any and everything they please and, their rights will protect them.

According to Webster, confusion means disorder. This bewilderment is a prevalent term that exists in many school settings. When confusion enters into the learning environment, it is difficult to teach the required subject matter. **Classroom Discipline without Confusion** will place order and clarity in your classroom. Simple techniques and strategies will allow you to get control and make teaching enjoyable, successful and fun!

Confusion and chaos have entered like thieves in the night to rob our classrooms of dignity and respect. We are losing some of our finest teachers, all at the expense of enforcing the rights of the children. Fighting, weapon possession, disobedience towards school rules, property and authority figures seem to be the order of the day.

Society seems to be in limbo, shock and it does not know what to do with children that are now out of control. Many people fail to realize many schools have disruptive children. Society wants the schools to teach all students regardless of what problems they have or from where they come. There is a scarcity of books on how to reach and teach these children many of whom do not want to be taught.

Classroom Discipline without Confusion addresses these issues and concerns. It takes a realistic look at the children that are growing up in today's society and tries to address their needs and learning patterns. It is filled with everyday survival techniques that can be used effectively in many classroom settings. The techniques given are not the conventional methods that most people use. They are creative strategies designed to teach the hard to reach. They are methods that sap the confusion from the environment, so you can quickly access any problems.

The first premise is to know that **THERE IS AN ANSWER!** There is a way to reach and teach the students I have just described. I have sixteen years of teaching experience. Those years involved teaching elementary, middle and high school children. Setting your learning environment in order is a major step. I should know, I teach physical education. I have to teach indoors, outdoors, and in inclement weather. Other times, I have to work in a portable, on the stage, in the classroom, or in the auditorium.

I am responsible for teaching over 300 children weekly. I may not be an expert to many people. However, if you will open your eyes, mind and heart to my words, then you will know I do love children; especially those who are hard to reach and teach.

I have become very successful at what I do best--**TEACH**! I am confident I have techniques that will help teachers become successful, if they will honestly start with themselves. This means teaching yourself to prepare your environment so it will look, feel and represent success at first sight!

Starting within, I have found that excellence; dedication, caring, honesty, enthusiasm, organization, love, respect and leadership will change most environments into one of success. It all starts with you! Stay organized and confusion will rarely exist in your classroom.

Over the years, I have undergone a great deal of introspection. Looking deep within myself I asked, "Do I really want to be a teacher?" This is a question many teachers will find themselves asking. I suggest you take the Teaching Survey Questionnaire to get an answer to this important question.

The survey that I developed will allow you to answer the question, "Can you **Teach, No Matter What**" openly and honestly. I developed the survey to determine whether to remain in the teaching profession. After personally completing the survey, I decided to stay! However, I realized I could not continue to use the same methods that were given to me during my college years.

The children of today are very different and have special needs. These special needs evolve from different personalities and ideals that are difficult to understand and to address. Once reached, these are the most intelligent, gifted and talented students I have ever seen. Many possess natural abilities that if properly nourished can enhance our society.

I know I am only one person, but I have made a difference. I see in students what others constantly overlook. I try to reach the unreachable, because someone did the same for me. Now, I have a Master's degree. However, when I was in elementary school, I could barely read. Throughout my educational years with inner city schools, teachers who made a difference in my life touched me.

Collectively, the difference was classroom management. The classroom was decorative and colorful. When you entered the environment, the teacher was prepared to teach. The teacher was organized, dedicated, creative, energetic and excellent at his/her craft. These qualities eliminated the confusion from the classroom and allowed learning to take place. These techniques showed me that the teacher really cared.

As it was with my former teachers, so it is with me. Come now and journey with me through Classroom Discipline without Confusion. Then see if this book will help, you reach children that desperately need you!

Joy Williams

CHAPTER 1
Make a Decision to Teach, No Matter What

This time in life can be very stressful, if we allow it. I have written this book about classroom discipline to help teachers alleviate some of their stress. You must first make a decision about the profession that you have chosen.

Being a physical education teacher is a unique experience! Not only do I teach the physical aspects, but the educational components as well. For example, when teaching the side-step dance movement, I not only have to demonstrate the skill, but I am also required to use a visual aid to spell it. This would not be a problem if my classroom were not located outside. It is challenging to teach with the wind blowing away your chalkboard; or making sure all twenty-five students can hear directions with traffic constantly passing in the background. It is also difficult to teach twenty-five students a successful tennis lesson in a portable.

Teaching physical education is not easy. Many times, I would not have the facility, space or the material to produce the quality program, which was expected. Like classroom teachers, I have to display my students' work, but in the performance arena. This event is usually called May Day or Field Day involving all the students I teach.

In the beginning, I was very frustrated and overwhelmed with the conditions which I faced daily and what was expected of me. I felt my teaching ingredients were poor. That is why I continued to see poor results with my students. The teaching ingredients I speak of are low self-esteem, frustration, inexperience and confusion. My teaching situation did not allow me to be stable but mobile. I had to travel to five different schools within a week. It was difficult for me to carry my office supplies and equipment in the back of my car. Yet I did. It was not unusual for me to teach over 300 students a week. Like the classroom teacher, I was responsible for keeping accurate records and grades. Not only were my personal ingredients going into the mixture, I had to consider the students I taught. I had to find a way to take all these components to produce a successful product. The question became, **HOW?**

When society is filled with confusion and chaos, we should not be disappointed, frustrated, outraged, perplexed or overwhelmed when we have students sitting before us who are filled with the same ingredients. The majority of students being taught are by-products of a society that has many conflicting ideals. We must remember as we teach: what goes in will come out!

As you continue to read, silently ask yourself the following questions and make a decision about the teaching profession. Be sure to be honest with yourself. Answer with brutal frankness, or you will only hurt yourself. If the choice is to teach, then most of your answers should be yes. Many teachers will skip this section and many will pretend," I know I want to teach". Others will say, I was **"called"**, **"chosen"** and **"destined"** to teach. Yet, truth and honesty is what we instill in our students. It is called **VALUE EDUCATION.** Again, I ask you to take the survey and **MAKE A DECISION TO TEACH, NO MATTER WHAT!**

TEACHING SURVEY QUESTIONNAIRE

- Do you love children and see them all the same?
- Do you feel you can teach and reach all children?
- Can you see the positive outcome of a disruptive child?
- Do you respect the children you teach?
- Can you tolerate constant forms of negative behavior?
- Are you good at documenting?
- Are you able to handle and store mounds of paperwork?
- Are you open to new ideas and suggestions?
- Are you a self-starter?
- Are you a "go-getter"?
- Are you organized?
- Are you flexible?
- Are you a good listener?
- Are you success minded?
- Are you good at meeting deadlines?
- Can you work under pressure?
- Can you handle stressful situations?
- Can you handle irate parents?
- Do you feel safe in your work environment?
- Are you familiar with the policies and laws that govern the school district?
- Can you work well with authority figures?
- Can you follow rules and regulations?
- Are you familiar with and involved in the community you serve?
- Are you good at networking for resources that you need?
- Are you computer literate?
- Will you work until the job is done?
- Are you in good physical health?
- Do you have fun when you are NOT at school?

I hope that you answered yes to most of the questions. If not, you need to reevaluate your teaching career. For me, this decision was easy. The human investment was too great to be denied. I felt I was **"called"**, **"chosen"** and **"destined"** to teach. My **decision** was final!

CHAPTER 2
The Choice is Yours

I teach children from the inner city. They are constantly surrounded with a world that makes a joke of the educational system. They feel it is more important to be rich and famous than it is to learn to read and write. They take what they see--, which is mostly negative-- and bring it to school. Most of them feel their behavior is normal.

One mode of thinking is not being alarmed at what you hear or see children do. Most of the behavior is not necessarily directed at you; but is only a reflection of the patterns and lifestyles of our society. Many children are displaying behaviors they have seen at home, either in their community or on television.

Many raise themselves, while others live in conditions that are too horrible to mention. By the time they reach school, they have been involved in or surrounded by situations we would not believe. In school, teachers try to tune out the outside world and teach the students like children without regard for their background or environment. Many teachers do not realize we compete with so many technology devices. The children learn their favorite songs from singers, dancers and rappers using videos. Yet, some cannot read a paragraph. They wear all the latest shoe designs and clothing attire, but some cannot write a complete sentence. They can tell you what is going on in the music industry, but many cannot spell the name of their favorite artist.

By making the choice to teach, I began to answer the questions located in the survey. I realized I identified with my students. I would sit quietly and watch them. I pretended I was seven or eight years old and was being raised in 1998. For example, when I first started teaching I too was afraid. I needed someone to listen to me when things did not go well. I watched as many children were ignored or pushed away as they tried to explain their problems. I felt my heart sink as they moved from place to place as many of their peers laughed at their clothing. I would hear the conversations ring out saying, "Where are your brand name shoes?" I can only imagine trying to learn when sadness looms all around. We all know the problems although; there are few solutions being offered. Classroom Discipline without Confusion is an alternative arena for offering solutions. It will allow you to **"Set Your House in Order."**

CHAPTER 3
Remove the Confusion; Set Your House in Order

To keep my classroom free from confusion, I developed a detailed organizational plan. My concept was, if I removed most of the confusion and chaos; then I would have **ORDER!**

Order is needed in every facet of my workday. To be successful, I asked myself what I could do to help my situation. First, I started with a **successful attitude**. I decided I would create an atmosphere and classroom of success. I stopped looking for anyone to help me and I depended on the resources that I personally created in my life. During the summer, I sat down and created my plan. The plan entailed dividing my year into sections such as:

- Lesson plans
- Classroom inventory
- Equipment
- May Day
- Activity sheets
- Accident forms
- Discipline forms
- Meetings
- Workshops
- Grades
- Student folders
- Attendance

I dissected my school year to the minute detail. I looked closely at what was required of me for the next 190 days. I did not want to leave any stone unturned! Time was a commodity I took very seriously. Because when the school year started, I wanted to have my house in order!

With the presence of the students, beginning of the year responsibilities and deadlines, confusion would be an unwelcome visitor. Therefore, it is imperative to remove the confusion, by placing order into your classroom.

The house I speak of is my mindset. Being able to relate calmly to the students is very important. The mindset is made calm by having all materials ready for the day. I looked at my classroom and found ways to save time and space. For example, I used notebooks and plastic inserts to house all-important documents. Things I wanted to distribute to students could be quickly copied as needed. Before class, I could pull a copy from the notebook, reproduce the form and have it ready for my students. This concept saves space because I only house the forms that are needed for the school year.

I use two options in setting my house in order. Coming early and preparing my activity space sets the physical house. The next option involves my students. I use eight students who are known as **"Squad Leaders"**. They are randomly selected at the beginning of the year. They are very proud to lead the exercise and give me a verbal report of any misconduct. Their job is to lead the class in an exercise routine. They also assist me in setting my physical environment. For example, I let them know what activity will be performed and they place the equipment in the designated location.

The design of the activity court is already color-coded: White circles for the girls and black circles for the boys. If basketball is the activity, the girls stand in the white circle and the boys stand in the black. After receiving their equipment, I give a command. The verbal command for spacing out is called position one and two. The verbal command for knowing the objective for the day is called a chant.

Confusion usually begins when the environment is out of order. I have used color-coding to get order within my classroom and on the field. Children like colors. Outside my portable door, I have spray painted numbers and alphabets on the cement. When the children come to my door, they stand in designated locations before entering the portable. This is an excellent technique for taking roll or handling discipline problems.

There are eight squads. The children line up behind their squad leader and place their hands in position one and two. Position 1 has the arms in front. Position 2 has the arms to the side. This is a verbal command that allows students to have ample space when lining up. My roll book is correlated with the squad formations.

I have four simple words I use and enforce daily. At the beginning of the class period, I implement this technique. These words are very powerful if used properly. It allows the students to quickly chime in together and focus on me.

At the conclusion of saying the four words, I ask the students what the objective means. Together they will say, "What we're going to do today". This allows those looking or listening, as well as those I teach, to know what is going to happen next.

This is a very impressive tool for cutting down on confusion and it looks good when you have visitors. The technique shows you are truly organized and have control! The four powerful words that will set your house in order have the teacher leading the chant and the students following. Therefore, active participation is visible.

The four powerful words are:

TEACHER SAYS...	STUDENT RESPONDS/TOUCHES...	
Touch your head	THINK	HEAD
Touch your ears	LISTEN	EARS
Touch your eyes	LOOK	EYES
Touch your mouth	TALK	MOUTH

Being consistent is very important in eliminating confusion. I constantly supervise and guide the students into the objectives. I provide the tools, which will make the classroom effective, fun, and organized without confusion.

CHAPTER 4
Organize Your Classroom

Organization is not a very popular term among many. It is easier and more comfortable to keep things as they are, than change. For me, this is my strongest trait. I feel this characteristic alone has thrust me into the forefront of the discipline arena.

One cannot be effective if there is no organization. We see organization all around us. It begins in the classroom with taking attendance and continues throughout the day. There are no shortcuts to organization. If it is to be effective, it must be implemented properly.

I explain my organizational plan to my students' ages six to eleven. They are an integral part of my success, so they are always included. When they know the objective and what is expected of them, a lot of confusion is removed. However, as the "captain" of the ship, I must follow my plan closely. If I need to change, delete, update or remove "any" part of the plan, then students must be informed.

I explain, show and give examples of the information I want to discuss. These include procedures, behavior contracts, rewards, seating arrangements, equipment distribution, activity auditions and testing procedures. Most procedures are explained during the beginning of the year, but I introduce them throughout the class sessions. I review the procedures on a regular basis and entertain questions--yes questions! I allow my students to interact in the learning process.

I incorporate Value Education components while teaching the importance of being organized. I use examples of several businesses, which are located in the community. When introducing a lesson, I correlate it to something with which they are familiar. I explain the importance of patience. When learning a new physical education skill, I ask them to be **patient** when it is not their turn. I ask do they have to wait in line with their parents at the grocery store. When they answer yes, I tell them it is called **patience.** Just like their parents, they must learn to wait also. I correlate learning to read and write with learning their fitness skills. I explain if they cannot read the information on the fitness handout, they will not be able to complete an application. Reading and writing are important tools when obtaining employment. The children I teach may be young, but they can understand anything if you **teach** it properly; but it takes **patience!**

Once I draw similarities of my classroom to their daily experiences, many have a deeper understanding and appreciation for my objectives. By closely meshing Value Education within the curriculum, I am able to receive respect from hard to reach students. I accept where they come from and try to understand how they feel. I explain my objectives and try to elevate them to a higher level of thinking. This is not always easy.

I constantly look for opportunities to praise, inspire and encourage my students. If I have outside activities prepared, but instead use the portable; I explain. Normally, the weather is inclement and the activity has to be moved indoors. As adults, we know how this can affect a program and the classroom is no different. After explaining and apologizing, I entertain questions or try to diffuse any ill feelings.

The students know I am sincere when I speak, so many times, they understand. I thank the students for adapting to the change and provide treats at the end of class. Again, it is organized! I have a helper distribute the treats. The Treasure Chest is a box of individually wrapped treats. Students may also select from an array of other items like pencils, stickers and folders. By allowing the students to select their own treat, the discipline problems are limited. If the class did extremely well, I give a pickle or a pizza party during their lunch period.

I explain and inform all persons of my reward system to make sure there is not a problem. This keeps my organizational plan free from confusion. Communication is vital to the success of my program. When students take a written test, I review, give homework sheets and announce the test day. I always identify five students to assist with testing. They are organized to perform the following tasks: distribute tests, folders, pencils, and colored testing pens.

I place the class under standardized testing procedures. I announce the objective. I explain the directions, entertain questions, give examples, set a period and use a clock. I use colors for my test. For example, the fitness test is blue, the bubble sheet is white and the answer key is yellow. The colors are used for easy identification, distribution and organization.

To teach the value of trust, I allow the students to grade their own papers. The students place their pencils on the floor next to their desks. The colored pens are used to check their answers. ALL pens are the same for easy identification. I use a transparency and overhead projector to review the answers.

Each student has a copy of the answers, as I perform an oral review. This helps advanced students move ahead if I am going too slowly. By using this technique, the students receive immediate feedback to their grades. If they know in advance, where they stand in my class, it decreases confusion.

I re-check the papers and next class period inform the class of following all test-taking rules. I individually notify the students who incorrectly graded their test. I inform them they are not allowed to grade their papers for a few weeks. Having placed the Value Education component, honesty, in my organizational plan helps to limit this problem. Confusion is kept to a minimum by constantly reviewing, and updating my organizational plan with my students.

CHAPTER 5
Network To Success

Much of my success is due to the equipment and material I possess. Most of it belongs to the school; however, a great deal is mine. While making my organizational plan, I created a "wish list". These were items I needed to take the confusion out of my learning environment. I have found networking to be a vital part of my survival. I simply trade my services to get the material and supplies I need. I use my computer, teaching, and organizational skills to help obtain items on my "wish list".

This list includes the materials I networked, bought, requested through donations, sought through family, and loved ones, friends and community organizations. I have been able to receive the materials on the list because I am excited about being organized!

It was not easy to convince others to give me items I needed. Even so, with persistence and enthusiasm, coupled with a positive attitude, I accomplished miracles! I wrote to different companies and explained my dilemma. I asked for donations and many companies honored my request.

For holidays and my birthday, I asked family and friends for help. Instead of gifts, I asked them to give me an envelope with $25.00. This money was used to buy items for my classroom, or to pay college students to help with my classroom activities.

I make sure all supplies are easily displayed for all students. Upon entering my classroom, most materials are visible and ready to be distributed. Many teachers look for all their materials to come from the school district, but I do not. I have found the most successful way to get what I need is to "network". I know that money may not be available to assist with my needs, so I use other resources.

Networking is very easy for me. I think of the people that I know and call to ask for help. Most of them are so amazed at what I ask for; they give it to me. For example, my mother is an excellent cook! She can make chicken wings that will make you cry, because they are so good. I asked her to make 100 wings for my gymnastic team and she said yes! This saved me a lot of money!

I contacted a friend who is an engineer and asked him to put up three tents on May Day and he said yes! The tents were used to shade our volunteer workers. He took off work, arrived at 6:00 a.m. the day of the event and put up all three tents, free of charge! All I did was ask!

Having a pleasant personality is so important in networking for your materials and supplies. Whatever kindness is extended to me, I immediately send a thank you note. I am always thankful and grateful for donations or assistance rendered, because it was more than I had!

REQUIRED 'WISH LIST' CLASSROOM MATERIALS

1. Computer
2. Software
3. Cartridges
4. Electric pencil sharpener
5. Notebook paper/Graph paper
6. Ink pens
7. Markers
8. Folders
9. Clip boards
10. Overhead projector
11. Transparencies/with pens
12. Colored coded numbers
13. Spray paint
14. Handouts
15. Computer-generated tests
16. TV/VCR
17. 100-foot extension cord
18. Cellular phone
19. Megaphone
20. Stop Watch
21. Cones
22. Whistle
23. Envelopes/Stamps
24. Folders/Crates/Boxes
25. Balloons
26. Stapler
27. Staple gun
28. Tape recorder/Cassettes/CDs

I asked friends to donate items at their home they did not use or want, so I could enhance my teaching environment. Slowly, I accumulated the listed items, which have given me the edge to eliminate unnecessary confusion in my classroom. I make certain I have enough equipment to distribute to each student. This deters fighting, screaming, pushing, and ill feelings that occur when there is not enough equipment for everyone.

CHAPTER 6
Computer Wizard

Before there were computers, there were typewriters. As someone who is not afraid of change, I learned to master the computer. Systematically I moved through the field of technology with ease and success. I began to use the computer for everything from personal items, like my grocery list, to professional usage, like my lesson plans.

As my confidence and knowledge grew by technology, so did my skills. I began implementing computer-generated forms into my curriculum! I could cut, paste, create, edit and design all of my documents using the Macintosh platform.

Most times, I do not have time to detail behavior problems, so I created "Discipline Forms". These forms could be used in a flash. All I need to do is check the inappropriate behavior, review it, have student sign and place it in the mail. To my amazement, my discipline problems began to decrease. My friends began to call me the "Form Queen". If a student sneezed, pushed, hit or touched another student, I had a form. It became an obsession. Most times the forms were held in the student's folder, so many problems were handled in class.

The forms are listed in the Appendices. They are good to have when time is of the essence! The more discipline problems I encountered, the more forms I created. The forms are unique because they address the unique situations of today's children.

One form, listing different locations, can be used on the student throughout the day. For example, I can send a form to the Homeroom Teacher, the Supply Teacher, the Bus Driver, and the Media Specialist, the Cafeteria Staff and so on. The form lists the student's name and the inappropriate behavior that was performed at the designated location. For easy access, the phone number is listed if needed.

At the end of a week, I collect the forms. I meet with the student and show them their folder. To their surprise, it is filled with different documentation. It becomes a powerful tool to deter discipline problems. The student and parent, if necessary, will see the behavior pattern. It is very effective because you have several individuals documenting their behavior.

Using Value Education components to weave the importance of honesty, I explain in detail my discipline forms to the class and their purpose. I tell them they were created to keep confusion out of the classroom by documenting behavior.

I explain these forms are needed because the laws have changed according to how we could discipline in the classroom. I define corporal punishment, which means we are not allowed to touch them. I then explain the beauty of technology and how it is used in documenting their behavior. My computer portfolios house over one thousand pieces of information. Part of the information includes my lesson plans. These plans help me plan my lessons effectively.

My classroom routine involves using computer-generated handouts. The physical environment is prepared before the students arrive. The handouts list the objective and the activity for the day. For example, the students would perform their exercise routine, then walk or jog around the track. I used straws to determine the correct number of laps completed.

The students then have to perform a cool down routine and prepare for the activity of the day. They would play a fitness game and end with a quick review. This technique proved to be invaluable. The students know the objective and the routine for the day whether they are indoors or outdoors. By using computer-generated handouts, the students realize I am professional and organized. These handouts are used to give tests, introduce songs, dances, rules, consequences and rewards.

My handouts are used to review my rules. They are "think", "look", "listen" and "talk" to me if you do not understand. I always give respect no matter what is given to me. I explain to my students they have a choice to learn **the lesson** I have prepared or to be prepared to learn **a lesson.** The lesson for the student to learn is in the form of a document. The document describes the student's off task behavior, the location, the time and date. With Value Education in place, most students sign the form.

The computer-generated forms are easy to use and implement. I use carbon paper. I mail the top part to the parents and mail the bottom part to myself. Most times, I follow up with a phone call. If the parent did not receive the copy, I set up a conference. At the conference, I list positive attributes of the student. I then ask the parent for their help in trying to understand their child's behavior. I also ask for suggestions or solutions in curtailing inappropriate behavior.

I explain my document procedures to the parent. I explain why I mail a copy to **MY HOME ADDRESS.** The unopened envelope has codes on the outside. The codes are for the child's name, date, behavior infraction and what they wore to school. When a parent says they did **not** receive the document, I show them mine.

According to the United States Post Office, this envelope is an official document. When opened, the form reveals the child's signature and lists all the information I mentioned **BEFORE** the document was opened. The clothing code simply details how thorough I am in my pursuit to have order in my class!

After the meeting, many times I have few class disruptions. The students sense I am serious about discipline in my classroom. I will do whatever is necessary within my legal rights to eliminate confusion. If I show the parent how thorough, professional and organized I am, usually I do not have further problems. **Consistency** is the key to my success. By being organized and documenting everything I do, I normally eliminate a lot of confusion.

CHAPTER 7
Discipline at its Best

There will be times when some or all of your students will not want to do what is required. It will be days when not all the techniques you try will appear to work. These are the times you will have to individualize your discipline program, the **IDP.** Most people would agree that not all the students in the classroom are disruptive and some really want to learn. Identify those students who do not respect your program.

I begin my classes by calling students by their last name. It is amazing what saying Mr. or Ms. to a child will do. You must address each child with an open and honest heart. If you do not like children, they will sense it. Whatever you feel inside of your heart as you deal with children, they will respond to it. Respect is a two-way street. Respect for the students, usually leads to respect for the teacher.

I constantly talk to my students and ask them questions. I want to know is it anything they need before the lesson begins. I inquire, is the lesson too hard or too easy? I ask for feedback to let them know I am concerned. If a child is not on task, I will make certain I have done everything to ensure learning has taken place. For those hard to reach cases, I began a folder of their behavior. Using my computer-generated forms, I explain to the student the purpose of my observations.

I get information from other teachers to investigate the history and background of the child. This information gives me a closer look at the student I am teaching. I candidly and individually speak with the student away from their peers. I ask whether I have offended, disrespected or done anything wrong to warrant their disrespect. It is amazing that most will say no.

As I continue to document my observations, I may visit the home or the work location of the parent or guardian. I use my school I.D. and identify myself. I explain why I am at the home or work site and ask to see the parent or guardian. I extend my hand and apologize for coming, but express my concern as the reason for my visit. I begin with a positive report of the student and proceed to ask for help.

Most parents and guardians are concerned about their children. I present myself as a caring professional and many respond. I listen to their concerns, complaints or criticisms and record the information on my form. This is one technique, which has proven to be very effective however; I have others.

Students who are disruptive while I am teaching prove to be challenging. I have a list of phone numbers of the students in my class and, if needed, I use them. After several attempts to get the student to discontinue their disruptive behavior, I use my cellular phone.

I have friends that have "donated" **IDP** funds on my behalf. This money is donated and used to pay my cellular phone bill. While the student is in my presence, I call their parent or guardian. Since most are unfamiliar with my cellular phone number, they return my call immediately. I tell the parent or guardian that I apologize for taking time from their busy schedule. I introduce myself and explain the problem. I let the student talk and document the account. I place the form in their file for future reference.

To have a successful outcome, the income must be successful. I give all my students respect, until they show me they do not want it. As a professional, I try to investigate my actions. If I search and find I have done nothing, I **document, document** and **document** to find out who else can help the student.

If it appears my efforts are ineffective, I try one last thing. I visit, watch and document the child in various school settings. I will visit them when they are in one of the following locations:

1. Music class
2. Art class
3. Homeroom
4. Playground
5. Cafeteria
6. School bus

I take this documentation and show it to the student. I have a one-on-one conference with them. I explain that I am concerned about their behavior in my classroom. I explain that I want to understand and try to help them.

I also bring a trinket, or a peace offering to ask the student for their help. The trinket can be a certificate, a bag of potato chips, a folder or a pencil. This gesture would let the student know I am making one final attempt to understand their inappropriate behavior.

I use the Value Education concept and try to ask the student to be honest and tell me the truth about why they are being disruptive. I search their faces to find the answer and follow-up to get the parents' input.

The next class meeting, I do not pay attention to the student, yet I continue to document and keep files. After a short period, the student slowly starts to comply with my requests and begins to do as I asked. I immediately offer verbal praise in front of the class and a pat on the back.

I know this is a long and tedious process, but it works. There are no magic answers to the dilemma of discipline. All I can do is to continue to find ways to reach the students that are hard to teach.

CHAPTER 8
Customer Service

The trend today is accountability! More and more companies are moving towards the trend of outstanding customer service and the educational system is on the move. The system requires accountability, yet, many times, they fail to give the tools needed to produce excellence.

The previous survey was used to re-evaluate "who you are". In the beginning, perhaps you possessed a burning desire and a deep love towards the teaching profession. As time and society changed, so did the value system. The behavior of today is unacceptable as compared to years ago. The strategies used with children a few years ago will not work in many classroom settings today. For example, when a teacher asked you to be quiet, years ago, students quickly complied. Today, if you ask a student to be quiet, they will ignore you, continue talking, or tell you to shut up. This is where customer service concepts enter.

After many years of working with inner city students, excellence has always been at the forefront. There are diverse and unique circumstances, which surround teaching these students. I have tried, used and tested different techniques, which I found to be very successful. After I answered the teaching survey questions, I began to put excellence in motion.

The customer service department is one manned by the "human touch." This personalizes the business to the customers it serves. My business is to promote children of excellence, by achieving higher and higher levels of professional and personal standards.

Unlike most businesses, my products do not come perfected from the manufacturer. Instead, they are shipped as they are. It makes no difference how they are shipped, or how they arrive, **"I Will Teach No Matter What"**!

This is the philosophy, which has stood the test of time. With accountability on the increase, I arm my curriculum with fun, innovative and exciting material. My clients-- students--are my most important commodities!

I ask questions and thoroughly investigate when things do not go well. Unlike other teachers, I first look within. I do take it personal. I search my environment, my teaching strategies and materials to assess any weaknesses. Then I pursue whatever roads I need to produce my final process--**RESULTS!**

An example is setting the stage for a program. I either take the students given, or chose those I want. Next, I create the **RESULTS** I want. I network the supplies and materials needed and proceed to **TEACH** my clients. I explain thoroughly to the clients the **OBJECTIVE** and give them a time line. I ask if there will be any challenges to **DELIVER** what is desired.

I move next to **PRACTICE** and **PRODUCE** my outcome. I am not concerned about **MOTIVATION**, because I have already described their **REWARDS** and **INCENTIVES.** If they achieve what is required, then my job is done. The clients are inspired to produce because **MY WORD** is their **GUARANTEE.**

In business, having a "**track record**" is a good thing. In my profession, I have a record of accomplishment for producing results. I use business techniques to get the job done **No Matter What.** I do not accept projects that will not yield outstanding results. I will tell management what I need to succeed with a project and move from there.

Failure is a word **I** do not take lightly. If things do not go well in my environment, **I** investigate why. **I** only look at things **I** have control over. **I** look at what **I** can do to change and to make things better. **I** must keep this burning desire in my heart and mind, if **I** am to teach.

There are millions of variables, which say I cannot achieve what is required. There are millions of reasons, which say I should give up and quit. Millions say I should turn my back on the clients I serve and throw in the towel. The reason it is difficult is because of who and what I am.

I am excellent through and through. If you place me in **ANY** environment and in **ANY** situation, my faith tells me I **WILL** rise and **WIN.** Most of you will disagree, but it does not matter. What matters is what I think, what I feel and what I believe.

When I took the survey, the questions were already answered. I became the teaching survey when I was born. Born to win, born to teach no matter what the circumstances or the conditions. If you remove me from the teaching profession today, I will rise. It is not what is on the outside that makes me feel so special; it is my strong belief on the inside that makes it so.

Customer service is a way of life for me. I am so grateful to have the opportunity to touch and interact with young people. It is a pleasure to come to work and see which young person I can motivate each day. I go through the school day looking for a child to influence and inspire. I thrive on telling a co-worker to hang in there. I love to give encouragement to the individuals that pass through my teaching area daily.

It is an honor to be of service to the human race. Teaching for me spreads far beyond my 7:30 a.m. until 4:00 p.m. period. I wake up early to serve and go to bed thankful that I have served. Teaching, like life, is not drudgery to me. It is a gift to be shared and passed on to others. I do not waste my time, energy and thoughts about what I do not have. I am too busy trying to create **EXCELLENCE** from what I do have. These thoughts and ideologies will seem strange to many, but not to me.

Search yourself as you continue to teach day in and day out. Wake up and know the wave of the future is accountability. Like it or not, equipped or not, ready or not, here it comes and I hope you are prepared.

CHAPTER 9
Classroom Without Confusion,
The Winner's Circle

The winner circle is a circle that encloses you and you alone. This important chapter and shapes the core of your beliefs. To be a winner, you must start with yourself. This has been the theme for <u>Classroom Discipline Without Confusion</u>.

You must start with yourself and decide where you want to go. The decision is yours. No one can tell you, encourage you, or show you the way. You must decide for yourself. Teaching is not a profession that should be entered into for any other reason, except the strong desire to teach. It should not be entered into blindly. Once you have investigated the pros and the cons, make a choice.

Each year, you sign a contract that holds you responsible to perform certain duties. These duties are part of the **ENTIRE** contract and not to be selected at will. You made the choice to work through all the good and bad times. Once you have made the choice, begin to set your priorities.

Setting your house in order will help you achieve success. Your mind has to be made up, set and ready to remove all barriers. The summer should be your foundation. Getting all the materials and supplies that you need would help to alleviate stress, confusion and chaos once the school year begins. Once you know what to do--do it!

Your classroom is your arena, your home away from home. You must treat it as such. Organize and carry everything you will need to survive for the school year. Place those items that are inspirational and uplifting around. Bring in flowers and sweet smelling aromas that will carry you through the day. Stop and freshen yourself with goodies and fresh water that will quench your thirst, as you go back to the battlefield. Once you are organized, when it is time for duty, you are prepared and ready!

Begin to think of friends, family, and other organizations that believe in you. Many are eager and ready to assist. Secretly they stand and marvel at your tenacity and strength. Please ask for assistance. Many will be more than glad to help. Remove from your thoughts that you are alone. All the forces in the universe are at your disposal. Networking is a word that will be your friend. It will be a close companion in troubled times, but only if you ask!

I know you are afraid of technology, but you must become computer literate, if you are to survive. The 21st century is here and you must be prepared. Start taking technology courses that will allow you to work on FUN things. Once you become comfortable with technology, you can tackle the school requirements like lesson plans, schedules and grades. Remember you do not have to become a Computer Wizard, but you must start using technology.

Individualized discipline planning is essential. Not all students are your problem and some really want to learn. You must search and find creative ways to reach students. Rewards and positive reinforcement really do work. Investigate the history of the student that is not achieving your objectives, and document your findings. Parents and guardians can be of help if you approach the situation carefully.

High standards, accountability and customer service is the trend of today. Learn to take a good look at your students. See if you can see them as "clients". This approach will "soften" the hardness that surrounds them. This approach will allow you to see the potential that you did not see in the beginning. I know we cannot change the situation we are in, but many times, we can change our minds. Begin to find ways to succeed and win no matter what.

To be placed in the winner's circle, you must first think like a winner. If daily, you see darkness and destruction, ungratefulness and drudgery, change scenery. If this does not help, perhaps you have done all you can do. Maybe you have gone as far as you can go. Consider if you have served your purpose. There is so much that the human mind and body can endure. If you are not receiving acknowledgments and waves of appreciation, learn to create your own. Every human deserves praise and recognition and teachers are no exception. Find your place in the winner's circle. For me, it is a classroom that contains no confusion and few discipline problems. For me, this is where "success lies".

CHAPTER 10
Classroom Without Confusion, The ODEL System

I believe the Bible and what it says. I am never unsure that God is with me and will never forsake me. I feel this is the reason for my tremendous success using the **ODEL** system.

With this confidence, I rest assured knowing that if I am destined to succeed, God will create the opportunity. I rest knowing deep within that my destiny has been set and my mission in life is to help and serve others.

God has set a pattern, a plan, a time, and a place just for me. I am adamant not to allow anything to consciously distract and deter me from my **PURPOSE** or **MISSION**.

The ODEL System of Success

O RGANIZATION
D OCUMENTATION
E XCELLENCE
L OVING

The **ODEL** system is one that helps me survive on planet earth. It is a system that was birthed out of chaos and frustration. This system was created to put a cushion of softness within my heart, so that no matter what happens, it will never negatively affect me. When you teach, you must be able to deal lovingly with your surroundings, or you will become bitter. I prayed and asked God to help me to love with an unconditional heart and He answered with the **ODEL** system.

O represents being completely organized in all faucets of my life. It took years, but I placed order in my personal and professional world.

D represents my intricate ability to document the physical information, which confronts me daily. Once I view this information, I can make clear decisions.

E represents my commitment to excellence in all endeavors. I am always excited and eager to perform the task, no matter how big or small. By imprinting my endeavors with excitement, those who know me, will never be disappointed with the final outcome.

L represents the burning love I have for human existence. These love wells up deep inside my soul, and pours out like sunshine upon everyone I meet.

I always seek ways of implementing the **ODEL** system, but sometimes this is not always easy. Nevertheless, I smile and walk tall with the mindset that I am doing the best that I can to make daily situations pleasant and peaceful. I never worry about how the person is reacting or appreciating what I do for them, because I know that good always wins.

I live by this system. I try to avoid things that will cause me long periods of depression, sadness, concern, fear and doom. For this reason, I tenaciously limit the influx of negative and unappealing things that enter my mind, ears, heart and world.

I keep things organized at all times. This method is crucial so I can retrieve items quickly if needed. I allow myself a 24 to 36 hour turn around time to complete required projects. I make a list and check it twice to make sure I am not bombarded with too many responsibilities and obligations. Knowing your limits is a vital key to being successful.

I search and make sure my responsibilities are all God things and not **GOOD** things. Good things are nice to do, but they will not help me get closer to the **DESTINY** that God has chosen for me. My destiny lies in teaching those that are in need.

I am very successful in all that I do, think, and feel. My success has come, because I have placed the **ODEL** system in motion. I know that this **SYSTEM** was given to me to win and succeed in the game of life. You must spend lots of time, effort, and energy reading to achieve a high level of success. At this level, you will find that most of your time spent on earth is joyous and full of contentment.

Few people can admit they are happy most of the time. No matter where I find myself in life, it is a **GOOD** place, because I am **ALIVE** and in good health. All I have to do is apply the **ODEL** system to all my affairs and I will continue to achieve a high level of well being.

My attitude does not depend on how I feel; I am determined to **SEE** the **BEST** way of existing in the **CURRENT** situation. No matter what happens in my life, I will use the circumstances to my advantage. I believe and know the circumstances will make me stronger, wiser and more helpful to others that I meet on my journey.

If you want to take the confusion out of your life, try the **ODEL** system. It may be difficult to implement, but the rewards are awesome!

APPENDICES

ACCIDENT REPORT FORM

SCHOOL NAME _____
ADDRESS _____
CITY _____
STATE _____
ZIP CODE _____

This form is being prepared by: _____
Title:_____

The student listed below had an **accident**. This form is being prepared to make certain the student is okay. Every effort will be made to notify the parent/guardian of the **accident**. This form will be completed and held in a file for future reference.

Student Name   _____
Homeroom Teacher   _____
Grade Level   _____
Time   _____
Other Location   _____

Student:

Fell	☐
Became Dizzy	☐
Developed Cramp	☐
Developed Headache	☐
Complain of pain	☐
Developed Stomach Pain	☐
Developed Nose Bleed	☐
Other	☐

Comments and Details:

_____
_____
_____
_____

Teacher Signature   _____
Parent Name   _____
Parent Signature   _____
Phone Number   _____
Student Signature   _____
Date   _____

F-1

DISCIPLINE FORM (Art class)

SCHOOL NAME _____

ADDRESS _____

CITY _____

STATE _____

ZIP CODE _____

This form is being prepared by: _____

Title: _____

Student Name _____
Homeroom Teacher _____
Grade Level _____
Time _____
Other Location _____

Student:

Talking Loud ☐
Fighting ☐
Disrespecting Teacher ☐
Eating/Chewing gum ☐
Disrupting the lesson ☐
Talking after being moved ☐
Throwing objects in room ☐
Other ☐

Comments and Details:

_____

_____

_____

_____

Teacher Signature _____
Parent Name _____
Parent Signature _____
Phone Number _____
Student Signature _____
Date _____

F-2

DISCIPLINE FORM (BUS)

SCHOOL NAME _____

ADDRESS_____

CITY _____

STATE _____

ZIP CODE _____

This form is being prepared by: _____

Title:_____

Student Name _____
Homeroom Teacher _____
Grade Level _____
Time _____
Other Location _____

Student:

Running to the bus	☐
Standing up/Talking Loud	☐
Yelling out the window	☐
Playing/pushing others	☐
Fighting	☐
Disrespecting driver	☐
Hanging out the window	☐
Other	☐

Comments and Details:

_____
_____
_____
_____

Teacher Signature _____
Parent Name _____
Parent Signature _____
Phone Number _____
Student Signature _____
Date _____

DISCIPLINE FORM (Cafeteria)

SCHOOL NAME _____

ADDRESS _____

CITY _____

STATE _____

ZIP CODE _____

This form is being prepared by: _____

Title: _____

Student Name   _____
Homeroom Teacher   _____
Grade Level   _____
Time   _____
Other Location   _____

Student:

Pushing in line ☐

Talking/Playing in line ☐

Throwing food ☐

Disrespecting others ☐

Yelling ☐

Talking loud ☐

Jumping line ☐

Other ☐

Comments and Details:

_____

_____

_____

_____

Teacher Signature   _____
Parent Name   _____
Parent Signature   _____
Phone Number   _____
Student Signature   _____
Date   _____

F-4

DISCIPLINE FORM (Classroom)

SCHOOL NAME _____

ADDRESS _____

CITY _____

STATE _____

ZIP CODE _____

This form is being prepared by: _____

Title: _____

Student Name _____

Homeroom Teacher _____

Grade Level _____

Time _____

Other Location _____

Student:

Talking Loud	☐
Fighting	☐
Disrespecting Teacher	☐
Eating/Chewing gum	☐
Disrupting the lesson	☐
Talking after being moved	☐
Throwing objects in room	☐
Other	☐

Comments and Details:

_____

_____

_____

_____

Teacher Signature _____

Parent Name _____

Parent Signature _____

Phone Number _____

Student Signature _____

Date _____

F-5

OBSERVATION DISCIPLINE FORM

SCHOOL NAME _____

ADDRESS _____

CITY _____

STATE _____

ZIP CODE _____

This form is being prepared by: _____
Title: _____
Date: _____

PURPOSE

1. To carefully watch and observe student over a certain period.
2. To write and check off behavior that is inappropriate.
3. To thoroughly seek strategies which will help alter or cease negative behavior.
4. To seek outside assistance for the student whose needs may be beyond the teachers reach.
5. To investigate resources that will help the student stay on task.
6. To seek ways to help the student become actively involved and responsible during the learning process.
7. To empower and encourage the student to use self-control and help create a positive learning environment.
8. To review the observation form with the student to ensure that a 75% level of understanding and compliance is taking place.
9. To find successful ways to assist the student as they learn to interact with others.
10. To provide documentation for the parent/guardian during parental conferences.

Student Name _____

Homeroom Teacher _____

Grade Level _____

Time _____

Location _____

Teacher Signature _____

Parent/Guardian Name _____

Parent/Guardian Signature _____

Phone Number _____

Student Signature _____

Date _____

Student:

Singing/Talking to themselves	☐
Whistling/Humming	☐
Yelling out	☐
Using vulgar language	☐
Not responding when spoken to	☐
Turning away when adult is speaking	☐
Tapping on the desk	☐
Harassing others	☐
Spreading rumors about others	☐
Fighting/Pushing others	☐
Teasing/Bothering others (bullying)	☐
Pushing/Shoving others	☐
Not participating	☐
Not turning in assignments	☐
Not completing homework	☐
Receiving constant reprimands	☐
Creating constant class disruptions	☐
Other	☐

COMMENT BOX

Parent/Guardian Signature _____ **Date:** _____

Teacher Signature _____ **Date:** _____

Student Signature _____ **Date:** _____

F-7

ENVELOPE LABELS

To The Parents of:

_____
_____
_____
_____

To The Parents of:

_____
_____
_____
_____

To The Parents of:

_____
_____
_____
_____

To The Parents of:

_____
_____
_____
_____

To The Parents of:

_____
_____
_____
_____

To The Parents of:

_____
_____
_____
_____

To The Parents of:

_____
_____
_____
_____

EXCELLENT

CONDUCT AWARD

PRESENTED TO

_____

DATE _____

TEACHER _____

F-9

DISCIPLINE FORM (Field Trip)

SCHOOL NAME _____

ADDRESS _____

CITY _____

STATE _____

ZIP CODE _____

This form is being prepared by: _____

Title: _____

Student Name   _____
Homeroom Teacher   _____
Grade Level   _____
Time   _____
Other Location   _____

Student:

Playing on the bus	☐
Constantly talking on the bus	☐
Disrespectful during event	☐
Eating/Chewing gum	☐
Talking loud on the bus	☐
Disrespectful to others	☐
Fighting	☐
Other	☐

Comments and Details:

_____

_____

_____

_____

Teacher Signature   _____
Parent Name   _____
Parent Signature   _____
Phone Number   _____
Student Signature   _____
Date   _____

F-10

DISCIPLINE FORM (Hallway)

SCHOOL NAME _____

ADDRESS _____

CITY _____

STATE _____

ZIP CODE _____

This form is being prepared by: _____

Title: _____

Student Name _____
Homeroom Teacher _____
Grade Level _____
Time _____
Other Location _____

Student:

Talking Loud ☐
Fighting ☐
Disrespecting Teacher ☐
Eating/Chewing gum ☐
Disrupting the lesson ☐
Talking after being moved ☐
Throwing objects in room ☐
Other ☐

Comments and Details:

_____

_____

_____

_____

Teacher Signature
Parent Name
Parent Signature
Phone Number
Student Signature
Date

LATE PASS TO CLASS

Dear: _____

Please admit the following student(s) to class

_____

_____

_____

_____

Thank you so much for you cooperation,

_____
Teacher

Date: _____   Time: _____

DISCIPLINE FORM (Letter to Parent)

SCHOOL NAME _____

ADDRESS _____

CITY _____

STATE _____

ZIP CODE _____

This form is being prepared by: _____

Title:_____

Dear _____

I am writing this letter to let you know the reasons I did not follow the rules, which were given to me. The person who has me completing this form is concerned about my education and wants to help me do better in school.

I understood the rules and I had everything I needed, but the reason **I DID NOT** follow the rules was because:

_____

_____

_____

_____

_____

_____

These are the reasons I did not follow the rules. I will try to do better in the future because I know an education is very important.

Student Signature _____

Date _____

DISCIPLINE FORM (Media Center)

SCHOOL NAME _____

ADDRESS _____

CITY _____

STATE _____

ZIP CODE _____

This form is being prepared by: _____

Title: _____

Student Name _____

Homeroom Teacher _____

Grade Level _____

Time _____

Other Location _____

Student:

Running/Playing	☐
No Hall Pass	☐
On Computer Without Permission	☐
Eating/Chewing gum	☐
Not returning books	☐
Talking Loud	☐
Not obeying Library rules	☐
Other	☐

Comments and Details:

_____

_____

_____

Teacher Signature _____

Parent Name _____

Parent Signature _____

Phone Number _____

Student Signature _____

Date _____

F-14

DISCIPLINE FORM (MUSIC)

SCHOOL NAME _____

ADDRESS _____

CITY _____

STATE _____

ZIP CODE _____

This form is being prepared by: _____

Title: _____

Student Name _____

Homeroom Teacher _____

Grade Level _____

Time _____

Other Location _____

Student:

Talking Loud ☐

Disrespecting Teacher ☐

Not paying attention ☐

Eating/Chewing gum ☐

Talking after being moved ☐

Disrupting the lesson ☐

Not participating ☐

Other ☐

Comments and Details:

_____

_____

_____

_____

Teacher Signature _____

Parent Name _____

Parent Signature _____

Phone Number _____

Student Signature _____

Date _____

OBSERVATION DISCIPLINE FORM

SCHOOL NAME _____

ADDRESS _____

CITY _____

STATE _____

ZIP CODE _____

This form is being prepared by: _____

Title: _____

Date: _____

Student Name _____
Homeroom Teacher _____
Grade Level _____
Parent/Guardian Name _____

Address

Violations

1. Talking ☐
2. Playing ☐
3. Pushing/shoving ☐
4. Disrespecting others ☐
5. Not completing assignment ☐
6. Not completing homework ☐
7. Using inappropriate language ☐
8. Eating/chewing ☐
9. Constant disruptions ☐
10. Outbursts ☐
11. Pushing/shoving in line ☐
12. Disrespectful to an adult ☐
13. Disrespectful to classmates ☐
14. Other

Violation Number	Time	Date	Warning?	Did they stop?	Comments
			Yes/No	Yes/No	
			Yes/No	Yes/No	
			Yes/No	Yes/No	
			Yes/No	Yes/No	
			Yes/No	Yes/No	

F-16

OFF TASK CLASSROOM CHECKLIST

Week of _____
Teacher _____
Grade _____

Directions: Place a time next to the student's name. This indicates the **SUBJECT** and the **TIME** the student was off-task.
Use the **TOTAL** column for weekly progress reports.

Student's Name	Language Arts	Math	Science	Health	Homeroom	Total

F-17

OFF TASK OBSERVATION FORM

SCHOOL NAME _____

ADDRESS _____

CITY _____

STATE _____

ZIP CODE _____

Purpose: To find ways to help the student stay on task. Several subjects are listed. During the day, observations are made. The student is required to **COMPLETE** several assignments

This form will be used to **VIEW** what the student did **INSTEAD** of being on task during the required period. This form will be used **WEEKLY** to give parents an **ACCURATE** and **DETAILED** account of their child's **DAILY** progress. It will also be used to find alternative was to help student stay **ON TASK.**

Student Name _____

Teacher _____

Grade Level _____

Parent/Guardian _____

Phone Number(s) _____

Student:

Starring	☐
Excessive Talking	☐
Making loud noises	☐
Outbursts	☐
Playing with others	☐
Fighting	☐
Playing with toys	☐
Sleeping in class	☐
Incomplete assignments	☐
Throwing objects	☐
Noise distractions	☐
Eating/Chewing gum	☐
Grooming during class	☐
Other	

Date _____

F-18

OFF TASK CLASSROOM TALLY SHEET

Week of _____
Teacher _____
Grade _____

Directions: Use the **TOTAL** column for weekly progress reports.

Student's Name	Language Arts	Math	Science	Health	Homeroom	Total

F-19

DISCIPLINE FORM (Restroom)

SCHOOL NAME _____

ADDRESS _____

CITY _____

STATE _____

ZIP CODE _____

This form is being prepared by: _____

Title:_____

Student Name _____
Homeroom Teacher _____
Grade Level _____
Time _____
Other Location _____

Student:

Yelling ☐
Putting paper on the floor ☐
Staying too long ☐
Constantly needing to be excused ☐
Throwing/splashing water ☐
Defacing/Damaging school property ☐
Playing ☐
Other ☐

Comments and Details:

_____
_____
_____
_____

Teacher Signature _____
Parent Name _____
Parent Signature _____
Phone Number _____
Student Signature _____
Date _____

PHYSICAL EDUCATION DISCIPLINE FORM

SCHOOL NAME _____

ADDRESS _____

CITY _____

STATE _____

ZIP CODE _____

This form is being prepared by: _____

Title: _____

Student Name _____
Homeroom Teacher _____
Grade Level _____
Time _____
Other Location _____

Student:

Singing/Dancing	☐
Whistling/Humming	☐
Yelling out	☐
Using vulgar language	☐
Not responding when spoken to	☐
Turning away when adult is speaking	☐
Tapping on the desk	☐
Harassing others	☐
Giving the wrong name	☐
Fighting/Pushing others	☐
Teasing/Bothering others	☐
Pushing/Shoving others	☐
Not participating	☐
Not turning in assignments	☐
Not completing assignments	☐
Receiving constant reprimands	☐
Creating constant class disruptions	☐
Other	☐

Teacher Signature _____
Parent Name _____
Parent Signature _____
Phone Number _____
Student Signature _____
Date _____

DISCIPLINE LETTER MAILING LIST

The following students received discipline letters which were mailed

Today's Date _____

Student's Name	Mailing Address	Phone Number	Teacher

F-22

CERTIFICATE OF APPRECIATION

AWARDED TO

_____

FOR BEING A

FANTASTIC PERSON

TEACHER _____

DATE _____

F-23

SUPPLY TEACHER DISCIPLINE FORM

SCHOOL NAME _____

ADDRESS _____

CITY _____

STATE _____

ZIP CODE _____

This form is being prepared by: _____

Title: _____

Student Name _____

Homeroom Teacher _____

Grade Level _____

Time _____

Other Location _____

Student:

Singing/Dancing	☐
Whistling/Humming	☐
Yelling out	☐
Using vulgar language	☐
Not responding when spoken to	☐
Turning away when adult is speaking	☐
Tapping on the desk	☐
Harassing others	☐
Giving the wrong name	☐
Fighting/Pushing others	☐
Teasing/Bothering others	☐
Pushing/Shoving others	☐
Not participating	☐
Not turning in assignments	☐
Not completing assignments	☐
Receiving constant reprimands	☐
Creating constant class disruptions	☐
Other	☐

Teacher Signature _____

Parent Name _____

Parent Signature _____

Phone Number _____

Student Signature _____

Date

_____

F-24

Queen of Discipline Daily Sponge Survey

Name _____

Date _____

School _____

Grade Level _____

Please write and let me know have you had a good day, by answering the following questions.

• Have you been kind to everyone today?	Yes	No
• Did you get to work on time?	Yes	No
• Were you organized and had everything in order?	Yes	No
• When pressure is placed on you, do you remain calm and poised?	Yes	No

Please write and tell me from the above answers why you did or did not have a good day.

_____

_____

_____

_____

_____

_____

_____

_____

_____

_____

_____

_____

_____

Queen of Discipline Dream with Me
What is the perfect classroom setting?

Name _____

Date _____

School _____

Grade Level _____

Please write and let me know what a "perfect" classroom would look like if you could "dream" and have what you wanted?

1. What type of classroom do you envision as being conducive for learning? Be very creative. Include students, staff and the learning environment.

_____

_____

_____

_____

_____

_____

_____

_____

_____

_____

_____

_____

_____

_____

Queen of Discipline Dream with Me
What do you do to keep yourself fit to teach?

Name _____

Date _____

School _____

Grade Level _____

As you teach each day, you need energy and stamina to do all the requirements that are necessary in the field of teaching.

- Describe what you do to take care of yourself physically, and mentally. List exercises, spas, massages, walking, jogging, dancing etc.

_____

_____

_____

_____

_____

_____

_____

_____

_____

_____

_____

_____

_____

_____

_____

Queen of Discipline Dream with Me Form
Bench Mark to Excellence

Name _____

Date _____

School _____

Grade Level _____

Please write and let me know if you are where you expected to be in the teaching profession? I have used my timeline as a marker for you to use.

Ms. J. Williams	Your Name
1973 Graduated from Douglass	
1973 Tuskegee Nursing Major	
1975 Tuskegee P. E. Major	
1983-Present Atlanta Public Schools employee	
1990 Teacher of the Year	
1998 Book Written	
1999 2nd Book Written	
2000 Teacher of the Year	
Conclusion/Destined to Teach	

F-28

115

Queen of Discipline Music Forum

Name _____

Date _____

School _____

Grade Level _____

Please make a list of music you would use in your classroom to make the atmosphere suitable for your teaching style.

Also, tell why you would or would not **use music in your classroom.**

_____

_____

_____

_____

_____

_____

_____

_____

_____

_____

_____

_____

_____

_____

_____

_____

_____

Queen of Discipline Blindfold Mentality

Name _____

Date _____

School _____

Grade Level _____

Blindfold Mentality **is the ability to go in any room in your home, work, or vehicle environment and be able to pick-up any item you need with undo strain or stress. Example: You could blindfold me and I could go and get a pair of scissors from my desk area in the kitchen, could you? (Smile)**

Score: 1-3   Poor   4-7   Fair   8-13 Super

Please place check marks next to the areas that are so organized that you could find any item, even if you were blindfolded. Please, please be honest! (Smile)

1. **Classroom**   ☐
2. **Desk draw**   ☐
3. **Classroom closets**   ☐
4. **Roll Book**   ☐
5. **Student's desk area**   ☐
6. **House**   ☐
7. **Kitchen**   ☐
8. **Garage**   ☐
9. **Yard**   ☐
10. **Closet at home**   ☐
11. **Refrigerator**   ☐
12. **Bills (phone #'s, addresses)**   ☐
13. **Vital information (dentist, doctor, will, insurance policies etc)**   ☐

Queen of Discipline Documentation Information Form

Name _____

Date _____

School _____

Grade Level _____

Documentation **is vital to your survival as a teacher. You must learn to use the computer and generate forms that will assist you.** Please list your documentation techniques for the various school district requirements.

Example: For your grades   **Roll Book/Computer**

School District Requirement	Documentation Method
Lesson Plans	Template
Discipline Problems	Letters/Forms
Parental phone calls	
Student Attendance	
Student Achievement	
Teacher's Absences	
Office Correspondence	
APS Yearly Portfolio	
Staff Development	
Daily Lessons to students	
Parent Conferences	
Co-Worker Correspondence	
Equipment/supply needs	
Supply Teacher Lesson Plans	

F-31

Queen of Discipline Incentive Information Form I

Name _____

Date _____

School _____

Grade Level _____

Incentives/ Treats/Rewards are great ways to help you get your class to stay focused on your objectives. Please list your Incentives/Treats and or Rewards. **Explain why you use them, or why you feel they are not necessary.**

Example: On the elementary level, I used a "Treat Box". On the high school level, I used extra points and Community Service Hours.

_____

_____

_____

_____

_____

_____

_____

_____

_____

_____

_____

_____

_____

F-32

Queen of Discipline Schedule Information Form II

Name _____

Date _____

School _____

Grade Level _____

Various schools have schedules that may cause discipline problems.
Time Management **is crucial in the success or failure of your classroom. Please list the type of schedule you have and discuss any areas of difficulty with the type of schedule that is implemented in your school.**

Example: **I work on the block schedule, which is 90 minutes twice a week with four classes per day. This is challenging, if you have a large group and not enough supplies and material.**

_____

_____

_____

_____

_____

_____

_____

_____

_____

_____

_____

_____

_____

_____

_____

_____

F-33

Queen of Discipline Information Form

Name _____

Date _____

School _____

Grade Level _____

Various schools have schedules that may cause discipline problems.
Time Management **is crucial in the success or failure of your classroom.**

Please use the chart and write your daily schedule, list any problems you may have at various times listed.

Time	Subject	# of Students	Location	Problems

Queen of Discipline Plan Information Form

Name _____

Date _____

School _____

Address _____

_____

Principal _____

Phone Number _____

Grade Level _____

Use this form to create and design a Discipline Plan. Please use this form to jot down important information that will help you design and implement this plan.

Classroom Procedures

Classroom Rules

Classroom Consequences

Classroom Rewards/Incentives

F-35

Queen of Discipline Consequences Information Form

Name _____

Date _____

School _____

Grade Level _____

Consequences and forms for Discipline problems are vital to classroom management.
Please list your consequences if students are not following class procedures.
Explain why you use them, or why you feel they are not necessary.
Example: In my class, I first review all the rules and have students sign the Discipline form, which has parent information, I then use check marks for violations the student made with time lines.

_____

_____

_____

_____

_____

_____

_____

_____

_____

_____

_____

_____

_____

_____

Queen of Discipline Form Information

Name _____

Date _____

School _____

Grade Level _____

Listed below are a few discipline problems I have noticed over the course of my teaching career. Please add to the list.

Discipline Problem	Place a check, if you have a problem in this area
Talking	√
Playing	√
Chewing gum/Eating	
Sleeping	
Listening to CD player	
Bringing Toys/Magazines	
Not staying in seat	

Queen of Discipline Creative Activity and Equipment Form

Name _____

Date _____

School _____

Grade Level _____

Creativity is so important in teaching! You need to be able to captivate and maintain the attention of the students you teach.

Please list your activities and or equipment you feel helps deter discipline in your classroom. **Explain why you use them, or why you feel they are not necessary.**

Example: In my class, I always have"30" items, so that all students will have their "own" item. I try to make sure they are "all" the same, so no confusion will arise.

Item	Number	Reason
Boom Box/Private CD collection	1	For activities in the class
Home made Candy Cane Sticks	30	For dance routines
Pencils	30	For each student to write objectives
Electric Pencil Sharpener	1	To quickly have order in classroom
Clipboards	30	For gym area with no desks

F-38

MONTHLY CHECKLISTS

These monthly checklists will prove to be invaluable! You will be able to take a glance at what items are needed monthly therefore, seeing smaller portions of your entire year readily will enable you to eliminate stress and confusion. This checklist is used for the classroom and personal development requirements.

Benefits of using the Monthly Checklist are:

1. Saves time
2. Advance preparation
3. Keeps track of classroom priorities
4. View upcoming activities quickly
5. Assess needs and opportunities
6. Acquire ample teaching materials
7. Plan for human resources
8. Schedule timely activities
9. Prepare strategic lesson plans
10. Create seasonal bulletin boards
11. Computer-generated testing materials

M

MONTHLY CLASSROOM CHECKLIST

GRADE LEVEL:
MONTH: AUGUST

1. Lesson Plans   ☐

2. Bulletin boards   ☐

3. Class Rosters   ☐

4. Classroom Rules   ☐

5. Discipline Plan   ☐

6. Classroom Centers   ☐

7. Name Tags   ☐

8. Class Procedures   ☐

9. Homework Procedures   ☐

10. School Rules/Consequences   ☐

Notes:

M-1

MONTHLY CLASSROOM CHECKLIST

GRADE LEVEL
MONTH   SEPTEMBER

1. School Safety Procedures   ☐

2. Classroom Monitors/Leaders/Helpers   ☐

3. Daily Attendance/Roll Book   ☐

4. Student Writing Portfolio   ☐

5. Student Discipline Folder   ☐

6. Pre-Test/Post-Test by Subjects   ☐

7. Lesson Plans   ☐

8. Grade/Evaluation Scale   ☐

9. Homework Assignments   ☐

10. Building Tour   ☐

Notes: ***Bulletin Board Update (If needed)**

M-2

MONTHLY CLASSROOM CHECKLIST

GRADE LEVEL
MONTH   OCTOBER

1. Emergency Evacuation Chart ☐

2. Fire Drill Plan ☐

3. Tornado Plan ☐

4. Bus Rules and Procedures ☐

5. Homeroom Monitor Assignments ☐

6. Hall Pass Procedures ☐

7. Seating Charts ☐

8. Classroom Dismissal Procedures ☐

9. Deficiency Notices ☐

10. Teacher's Committee Assignments ☐

Notes:

M-3

MONTHLY CLASSROOM CHECKLIST

GRADE LEVEL
MONTH   NOVEMBER

1. Lesson Plans ☐

2. Attendance Count (20-Day) ☐

3. Thanksgiving Activities ☐

4. Cafeteria Rules and Procedures ☐

5. Posted Class Schedules ☐

6. Classroom Student Roster ☐

7. Bus riders and Walkers Roster ☐

8. Classroom Inventory ☐

9. Media Center/Audio-Visual Equipment ☐

10. Faculty Meeting Notebook ☐

Notes:

M-4

MONTHLY CLASSROOM CHECKLIST

GRADE LEVEL
MONTH   DECEMBER

1. Lesson Plans ☐

2. Holiday Program Activities ☐

3. Parental Information Packet ☐

4. PTA Information Packet ☐

5. Textbook Distribution Information ☐

6. Science/Social Studies/Math Projects ☐

7. Supply Teacher Packet ☐

8. Office/School Supply Ordering Procedures ☐

9. Classroom Dismissal Procedures ☐

10. Teacher Evaluation Observations ☐

Notes:

M-5

MONTHLY CLASSROOM CHECKLIST

GRADE LEVEL
MONTH   JANUARY

1. Lesson Plans   ☐

2. Classroom Testing Procedures   ☐

3. Field Trip Information Packet   ☐

4. Cafeteria Rules and Procedures   ☐

5. Discipline Plan   ☐

6. Media Center Procedure   ☐

7. Technology Procedures   ☐

8. School Fund Raiser Packet   ☐

9. Core Subject Meeting Notebook   ☐

10. Grade Level Meeting Notebooks   ☐

Notes: *Bulletin Board Update (If needed)*

M-6

MONTHLY CLASSROOM CHECKLIST

GRADE LEVEL
MONTH   FEBRUARY

1. Lesson Plans   ☐

2. Tutoring/Club Assignments   ☐

3. Black History Month Activities   ☐

4. Homework Assignments   ☐

5. Grading Charts   ☐

6. Valentine Programs/Activities   ☐

7. Pretest/Post-Test Samples   ☐

8. Update Student Portfolio   ☐

9. Update PR Folder   ☐

10. Student Disciplinary Referrals   ☐

Notes:

M-7

MONTHLY CLASSROOM CHECKLIST

GRADE LEVEL
MONTH   MARCH

1. Lesson Plans ☐

2. Parental Involvement Strategies ☐

3. Parent Conference Log ☐

4. School-Community Involvement Log ☐

5. Student Anecdotal Records ☐

6. Social Worker Referral Procedure ☐

7. Counselor Referral Procedure ☐

8. Class Procedures ☐

9. Homework Procedures ☐

10. School Rules/Consequences ☐

Notes:

M-8

MONTHLY CLASSROOM CHECKLIST

GRADE LEVEL
MONTH   APRIL

1. Lesson Plans   ☐

2. Office Referral Procedures   ☐

3. Accident/Injury Procedures   ☐

4. Field Trip Request Procedures   ☐

5. Permission Slip Procedures   ☐

6. Spring Break Procedures   ☐

7. Non-Progression Notification Procedures   ☐

8. Mid-Point Evaluation Reports   ☐

9. Student Transfer Request Procedures   ☐

10. Teacher's Duties and Responsibilities Checklist   ☐

Notes: ***Bulletin Board Update (If needed)**

M-9

MONTHLY CLASSROOM CHECKLIST

GRADE LEVEL

MONTH   MAY

1. Lesson Plans   ☐

2. May Day Activities   ☐

3. Update Class Roster   ☐

4. Update PR Folders   ☐

5. Textbook Checklist   ☐

6. Library Book Return Checklist   ☐

7. Uniform/Equipment Return   ☐

8. Final Examinations   ☐

9. Certificates/Awards Procedures   ☐

10. Calendar of Upcoming Events   ☐

Notes:

M-10

MONTHLY CLASSROOM CHECKLIST

GRADE LEVEL
MONTH   JUNE

1. Update Inventory Checklist ☐

2. Media Center/AV Equipment Return ☐

3. Bulletin board Removal ☐

4. Report Card Distribution ☐

5. Textbook Return Procedures ☐

6. Roll Book Return Procedures ☐

7. Graduation Procedures ☐

8. End of School Activities ☐

9. Classroom Key Return Procedures ☐

10. Thoroughly Clean Classroom ☐

Notes: *Pack and label classroom materials*

M-11

CLASSROOM DISCIPLINE WITHOUT CONFUSION
By Joy Williams

For Immediate Release:

Classroom Discipline Without Confusion

Is a tried and tested book filled with proven techniques that work!

Ms. Williams is currently a successful teacher in the inner-city school district in Georgia. She can handle large groups of students with little or no discipline problems.

Try this book for only $14.95, plus shipping and handling and watch it change your life.

This Book is available at:
Amazon.com, BarnesandNoble.com, Borders.com etc.

or

For more information or seminars:
Call Ms. Williams at (770) 507-7460
P.O. BOX 923
Stockbridge, GA 30281

TO HIS GLORY PUBLISHING COMPANY, INC.

111 Sunnydale Court, Lawrenceville, GA 30044, U.S.A.

(770) 458-7947

Order Form for Bookstores

Order Date: _____

Order Placed B _____

Address: _____

_____

City_____ ST/ZIP_____

Phone#:_____

Email:_____

Purchase Order#:_____

By fax:

By phone:
  Terms:

Discount:
  Return Policy: Within 1 Year

Title and ISBN#	Quantity	List Price
Shipping Method:		
Media		
UPS		
FedEx		
Other (please describe)		

Ship To Address:

_____

_____

_____

_____

_____

_____

Bill To Address:

_____

_____

_____

_____

_____

_____

TO HIS GLORY PUBLISHING COMPANY, INC Use Only - Billing Information

Invoice No.:_____ Invoice Amount:_____ Invoice Date:_____

www.ingramcontent.com/pod-product-compliance
Lightning Source LLC
LaVergne TN
LVHW081316060426
835509LV00015B/1541